Ephesia ext

A Pra

John Proctor

General Secretary of the United Reformed Church

GROVE BOOKS LIMITED
RIDLEY HALL RD CAMBRIDGE CB3 9HU

Contents

Note

Commentaries mentioned in this Grove booklet are given in full detail at the end in a list of recommended further reading, and only brief footnote references are given through the book.

Acknowledgments

The photograph of the author on the back cover is by Chris Andrews. A small amount of the material in this book has been previously used in a URC periodical and is used here by kind permission of the publisher.

First Impression December 2018

ISSN 1365-490X

ISBN 978 1 78827 068 7

Ephesians With or Without Context?

1

Ephesians stands apart among Paul's letters. The language and tone constantly reach for the sky. Exalted turns of phrase highlight the power of the gospel and point emphatically to the majesty of God. Yet Ephesians does not seem to interact tightly with specific problems in its readers' lives in the ways other New Testament letters do. So what kind of letter is it, and what might be the pastoral and practical payoff of using this kind of elevated language?

This booklet will discuss two kinds of answer to that question. Then it will reflect on the relevance and value of Ephesians to the people who read it first, and on insights and challenges it brings to the church today. Along the way we shall dip into most of the text and discuss the main themes and ideas that appear in it. We shall look at some difficult questions that the letter raises, and at some challenges and invitations it puts before our own Christian living.

First to two broad streams of approach to the question mentioned above: what sort of letter is Ephesians, and why was it written in this way?

After Paul

One view suggests that the letter postdates Paul's lifetime by a decade or two. It was written as a summary of his teaching for a generation of Christians who had not known him. So you could liken Ephesians to the London Eye.[1] It gives you an overview of Paul's theology. At that stage in the church's life it seemed important to distance Paul's thought from any particular time-bound or local situation, and to release what he had said to quite a wide Christian public.

The argument for reading Ephesians in this way goes as follows:

1 The words 'in Ephesus' are absent from a few ancient manuscripts including three of the oldest (1.2). Admittedly, the phrasing 'To the saints who are…' might presume a place name, and no other place name appears in any manuscript. Yet 'Ephesus' is not there in them all. Has it been taken out to make the letter seem more general? Or was it never in, because the letter was always intended to be general?

2 The writing style is more elaborate than Paul usually is. Long sentences, grand strings of nouns, elevated rhetoric—it is not quite

what we are used to from the argumentative man who wrote Galatians and 2 Corinthians, for example. Nor is all the vocabulary typically his, if these more contextual and specific letters indicate the store of words he habitually used.

3 Paul's personal engagement is not so obvious in Ephesians. In some of his letters he says much about his circumstances and interacts quite acutely with the concerns and doings of the readers. Ephesians is more measured, even detached, say some.

4 Some of the theology is more elaborate, especially the theology of the church, where a number of Paul's ideas appear in mutated or developed form when compared with his other letters. For example, the word *ecclesia* in Ephesians refers to the church universal, rather than the church local as it does in Romans or Galatians. The body of Christ in Ephesians is oriented to Christ as head, and this letter also speaks about the body growing, whereas other letters have a narrower focus, on the unity and diversity of the body's different parts. In Ephesians, the church as temple rests on Christ the cornerstone, with apostles and prophets as foundation; in 1 Corinthians the temple image is used in a simpler and more straightforward way. In Ephesians the church as bride of Christ—an idea rarely mentioned elsewhere in Paul—is used as an extended parallel to the marriage relationship. And with all the elaboration there is something general and almost abstract about the church in Ephesians, without the specificity found in some other letters about individual fellowships and their members.

5 There are some close parallels between texts in Ephesians and in Colossians; generally Colossians is simpler, Ephesians more elaborate. The longest exact parallel is the commendation of Tychicus, bearer of the letter (Col 4.7f; Eph 6.21f). But there are other shorter yet still striking parallels, for example between Col 1.25f and Eph 3.2, 9, or between Col 2.19 and Eph 4.16. There does seem to be some sort of link between the production of the two letters: either they came from within the same circle, or one uses the other as template and source.

For all these reasons, Ephesians strikes many readers as more likely post-Pauline than genuinely Pauline. It has been described as 'a letter of reminder and congratulation,' recalling for believers a decade or two after Paul's time the privilege of belonging to the church and using this recollection as a challenge to faithful discipleship.[2]

The above is not, in my view, the most plausible reading of Ephesians, and the next few pages will explain why. But if you disagree with me, I encourage you to think how you might view and use the letter according to your understanding of its origins and nature. You may feel that Ephesians offers a biblical warrant for using Christian insight flexibly as the years go by, for conserving tradition but also reworking it from one generation to another. You may think that releasing yesterday's thinking from yesterday's problems, as Ephesians might have done, can allow that thinking to address today's needs and questions in a relevant and contemporary way. If you are right about the origin of Ephesians, and I am wrong, that is surely part of the insight it can give us.

Letter to Ephesus

However—and this is the second approach—I interpret Ephesians as a locally targeted letter. There appear to be numerous links and allusions to the cultural background in the city and region of Ephesus. Some of the distinctions in theology, language and style between this and other letters may owe something to this local context, as well perhaps to a mature stage in Paul's thinking and career. So I would not be ready in the way that some would be to distance the letter from Paul. Indeed, a good deal of the background to the letter can be read out from Paul's visits to Ephesus in Acts 18 to 20. For even if Ephesians circulated in a broader area than the city alone, it can be credibly linked with that part of the world the Romans called Asia and we would call western Turkey. Several main themes emerge from that Acts account.

I interpret Ephesians as a locally targeted letter

Cosmopolitan

First, Ephesus was not an isolated place. It was a big city, with about two hundred thousand residents, probably the third city in the Mediterranean, after Rome itself and Alexandria in Egypt. Like a lot of cities, especially ports, it was quite cosmopolitan, and had plenty of contact with other parts of the Mediterranean world. This shaped the church that grew up there. Apollos arrived; his personal roots were in Egypt. Prisca and Aquila settled in Ephesus (Acts 18.24–28); they previously lived in Italy, and in Greece (18.1). Disciples of John the Baptist were in the area, so his teaching had come that far (19.1–7). John is usually thought of as launching a splinter movement, a wave of renewal, within the Jewish homeland. But his influence has reached here far beyond the Holy Land, in some way distinct from both the wider Jewish community in Ephesus and from what we would think of as more mainstream Christian life. All those influences, and all of those people, became part of the Christian community in Ephesus. That church was not culturally monochrome. Like any diverse church, it had much to gain from diversity, but that gain would only be realized if there were serious attention and commitment to unity and identity.

Secondly, the permanent population of Ephesus was ethnically mixed. Paul started his preaching in the Jewish synagogue (19.8). When he had to leave there, he went to the school of Tyrannus, a debating hall, more likely linked to the philosophical and educational traditions of Greece than to any religious ideology (19.9). Thus the gospel had an airing in both Jewish and Gentile settings. By this time, about AD 50, Jews had been in Ephesus for 300 years or so. They were an organized group, a significant presence in the community, round about ten per cent of the population. Yet they were to some degree resented, because they were granted special privileges—exemption from military service, permission to collect and transport the annual Temple tax for Jerusalem, freedom to assemble and to keep their ancestral laws.[3] Jews were a people who belonged and yet a people apart. Yet when the gospel took hold and groups of believers in Jesus began to meet, these were, it seems, drawn partly from people with a Jewish background and partly from among the Gentiles. Again, unity will be an issue.

Superstition and religion

Thirdly, in Ephesus a lot of people were interested in, influenced by, concerned about or afraid of the occult. How can you manipulate the unseen world to shape the world you do see? How will the unseen world manipulate you, if you are not careful? Spells, curses, secret magic passwords, incantations, ceremonies, charms and totems to wear—all of these could help you to secure good fortune, turn events to your advantage, do down your rivals, and carry you unscathed through a threatening world. Recall the bonfire of the books in Ephesus (Acts 19.18f). This was a big industry. One feature, however, that we might not have expected is the extent to which this feature of Ephesian society overlapped and intersected with Judaism. Acts tells us of 'itinerant Jewish exorcists (and) seven sons of a Jewish high priest called Sceva' (19.13f). First-century Judaism was not all austerity and law-keeping. There was a mystical tradition too, of heavenly visions and journeys. And one popular distortion of this was a dipping into magic.

In Ephesus a lot of people were influenced by the occult

Fourthly, there was Artemis, local fertility goddess turned patroness and protector of the city and its people. From almost any point of view, she was the principal player in Ephesian life and in the cultural influences that rippled out from the city. Everyone knew that Ephesus belonged to Artemis. Her worship, her magnetism, had given the place a reputation, and a series of lucrative twinning arrangements with cities in distant lands. A lively tourist trade resulted, with plenty of work for craftsmen, making souvenirs for visitors to take home. Artemis gave the city some its best architecture—a top goddess deserves fine buildings to be worshipped in. She shaped a good deal of the economy, created many of the employment opportunities, and directed the calendar of public holidays, festivals and sports events. She even ran a bank; the local savings and loan company used her temple as a strong-room, and thus traded under the goddess's patronage. Artemis reached across the town and across the earth.

More than this, Artemis reached into the unseen and occult world—into the dark side of reality. We have spoken about magic and mystery. Many would have seen this as territory she owned. People said that her image had fallen from the heavens. So the stars in their courses were a realm she was believed to rule, as were the fates and fortunes the stars controlled, and the influence these might have on you. The sky belonged to her, the world of spirits and of the dead, and the souls and anxieties of the people. This was a wrap-around culture. The claims of Artemis met you on every street corner and waited for you across the whole stretch of your life.

The claims of Artemis met you on every street corner all of your life

No wonder, then, that the riot in the Ephesian theatre that Paul caused—capacity incidentally about 24 thousand—which started as a threat to the trade in Artemis souvenirs, gained attention and traction through being seen as a personal insult to the goddess (19.23–40). It climaxed with a furiously chanting crowd. 'Great is Artemis of the Ephesians' (19.34). Civic pride was at stake, and prosperity, ideology and identity. Even though Artemis was not the only deity you could worship in Ephesus—other Greek gods and goddesses were honoured too—everyone knew that she was top. Challenge that at your peril.

Power

A final cultural feature of Ephesus, hinted at in the final verses of Acts 19, is the shadow of empire. Rome ran the Mediterranean. 'We are in danger of being charged with rioting for what we have done today' (19.40). Even the cause of Artemis does not mean that anything goes. There is a colonial power in town, calling the shots, keeping an eye on order. The governor of the province of Asia lived there. Ephesus was keen to be seen as loyal. The city wanted to build a temple as a centre for the worship of the Roman emperor, and Rome was careful to draw out tangible expressions of loyalty, before eventually granting permission in the 80s. Ephesus was a city owned from afar, a subject people in an imperial world.[4]

So here is a richly cosmopolitan town, with a clear ethnic divide running through the church, a lively undercurrent of occult involvement within the community, the totalitarian claims of Artemis and the grip of imperial control. How do you live as a Christian in that setting? What would you say to a church there? What values would you underline and emphasize in a pastoral letter? In the next chapter I set out some things that have struck me in Ephesians.

2

Features of the Letter

Strength

Strength is a major emphasis. If Artemis was a constant and obvious presence in town, and empire a power you could not ignore, this church surely feels overshadowed and outgunned by a dominant and assertive culture. Their community and their world are dominated by other kinds of power. Forces and fears are abroad in their land that have little room for the claims of Christ. In such a setting, neighbours might think you strange, eccentric, misled, out of step. You would be tempted to withdraw, keep safe company, mix only with like-minded friends. Christians were likely to run out of confidence, to fear they had little to offer, to be constantly on the back foot, always keeping their head down, sensing that their community danced to a rhythm other than theirs.

This may be why this letter speaks so plainly and often of the power of Christ, of the majesty and might of his resurrection and ascension. This language is not a power play for a well-positioned church, but a word of assurance for a fearful church, a fresh perspective for a people who might be intimidated by the systems within which they lived and in which they bore witness to a very different Lord. To say that God is greater than any threatening power, and that the Spirit shares God's strength with the church, is a big part of the letter's message and purpose.

This letter is a word of assurance for a fearful church

Three passages underline this theme. At the end of chapter 1, we read of God's mighty power at work in believers, the same strength that God put to work in the resurrection and ascension of Jesus, in giving him supremacy over 'every rule and authority and power and dominion' (1.19–21). There are no forces greater than the ascended Jesus. There is no call to cower or hide. There is nothing from which one need shrink in fear or inferiority. The heavens as well as the earth, the unseen realm as surely as the seen, not only the world before death but the world beyond, are under his power, and this is a power that he shares with the church. God 'has made you alive with Christ, raised you up with Christ, and seated you with Christ in the heavenlies' (2.5f).

The second passage is at the end of chapter 3, a prayer for the church to be 'strengthened with might by God's Spirit in your inner being' (3.16), for 'God is able by the power at work among us to do far more abundantly than all that we ask or think' (3.20). Christian spirituality in Ephesus is to include an expectant laying hold of the strength of God.

The third is the well-known passage about the armour of God (6.10–17). 'Be strong in the Lord and in the strength of his might' (6.10), in order that you may 'stand' (6.11, 13, 14). Again we read of superhuman powers ranged against the church—'the world rulers of this present darkness, spiritual hosts of wickedness in the heavenly places.' Again there is a clear affirmation that God's resources are enough—not for an aggressive battle, but for solid Christian resilience, for a faithful community that will stick to its calling, values and loyalties. Christians can be strong. They need not be afraid.

Unity

A second theme is unity, which surely has particular relevance in a racially divided church. Jew and Gentile: two parties; two backgrounds; two sets of cultural assumptions. And two significant passages about unity. In the latter part of chapter 2, the death of Jesus is described as a destructive act. 'With his blood, in his flesh, through his cross' he has broken down a dividing wall—the barrier of history, custom and law that kept Jew and Gentile apart (2.13, 14, 16). Instead of distance, access to God and to one another. In place of alienation, reconciliation. No longer separate, but united in one body. Unity is a gift. A second passage stresses unity as a duty.

'Keep the unity of the Spirit in the bond of peace.' The word 'bond' is no accident. Paul is 'bound, held in bonds' (4.1), and this same word describes the solid grip that true peace can have on human relationships (4.3). That requires practical nurture: 'humility, gentleness, patience, forbearance' (4.2). It also reflects shared belief, the things Christians have in common—'one God, one Lord, one Spirit, one faith, one hope, one body, one baptism' (4.4–6). With all this to unite us, Christians have no right to act as if we were strangers to one another and preferred to remain that way.

Holiness

A third theme in Ephesians is holiness. Religious language is used a good deal in this letter to describe the Christian life. The New Testament regularly uses the word 'saints, holy people' as a label for Christians, and it comes up several times in Ephesians (1.1, 15; 3.5, 8, 18; 4.12). We might think this casual—a common label, used almost subconsciously—were it not for a few passages that deliberately stress the holiness of the Christian community, as a people identified closely with the distinct and beautiful life of God. As with unity, it is a gift and a duty.

The idea of holiness as gift comes at the end of chapter 2. The church is 'one body' (2.16). Then the metaphor changes to the church as 'a holy temple, a dwelling place for God, founded on the apostles and prophets, with Christ Jesus as cornerstone' (2.20–22). That is a given. It is the church's identity.

What Christians are to do about it comes between 4.25 and 5.20. There is talk of a new way of being human, of living in the light, of not grieving the Holy Spirit, of Christ offering himself in sacrifice, and of life that is fitting for saints. When we unpack the practicalities, it seems that words are a big part of this: it matters that Christians watch their truthfulness (4.25), temper (4.31) and taste in humour, that speech be kept clean, decent, fair, honest and good-hearted (5.4). More generally there is a perception in Ephesians that life is holy ground. Ordinary hours and regular days are a God zone (5.8–14). Being 'filled with the Spirit' (5.18) is the invitation—a steady process, the consistent faithfulness of a life that knows and shows the holy goodness of God.

There is a perception in Ephesians that life is holy ground

If the power talk related to the totalitarian claims of Artemis and of empire, and the unity theme to the ethnic divide within the church, then perhaps this language of holiness has some relevance to the diffuse and cosmopolitan way the Ephesian church has come together. Whom do Christians belong to, when they all come from different places? Holiness underlines the church's belonging to God in Christ. It supplies an identity that speaks to the depths of each person's experience. Your life is God's life; you are a saint; together, Christians are a holy community.

The Wisdom of God

Finally, a theme that may particularly relate to the canopy of occult superstition and fear that lay heavy over Ephesus. How can anyone know the right signs and secrets to penetrate these mysteries? Or are you a constant victim, programmed by a world you can neither reach into nor get away from? Amid this anxiety, Ephesians speaks of the wisdom of God. Not so much a practical wisdom, as in Proverbs, but here a mystical and revelatory wisdom, of a God who can open the eyes of the human heart to understand the hope, power and presence of the risen Christ (1.18–23). This is wisdom that God means to communicate to earth and heaven through the church (3.9–11). So this thought of wisdom, flowing from God through the church to the world and the powers that shape the world, is surely a message that can speak into a culture weighed down by thoughts of manipulation, fear and control.

Ephesians—a pastoral, contextual, targeted letter. To a small church outgunned by a totalitarian culture, the supreme power of the ascended Christ; for a divided church, the gift and call of unity; in a cosmopolitan community, language of identity that transcends earthly roots and race; and amid a fog of occult superstition, a penetrating and dependable wisdom.

Questions

- Which reading of Ephesians do you incline to find more helpful—one that sets it specifically and locally in the shadow of Artemis, or one that sees it as a more general repackaging of Paul's ideas for wide circulation in a later generation?
- Which of the four themes in Ephesians outlined above would you think most important for your local church to grasp and be grasped by?
- Would your answer to the last question always have been the same, or has it changed with the years? How might it change in the next few years?
- Which feature of Ephesian culture strikes you as most relevant to the context where you live?

3

Questions in Reading Ephesians

Ephesians in the Revised Common Lectionary

The Revised Common Lectionary's Sunday calendar offers Ephesians over seven weeks in the summer of Year B.[5] It pairs these epistle readings with two readings from Mark 6 and five from John 6. However, since both gospels and epistle are used sequentially, one would not necessarily look for thematic echoes in these pairings. The detail of these lectionary weeks is in the middle column below, while the right-hand column shows a few other occasions in the three-year calendar when Ephesians is assigned.

Ephesians 1.1-14	Proper 10, Year B	Christmas 2, ABC
Ephesians 1.11-23		Christ the King, A
Ephesians 2.1-10		Lent 4, B
Ephesians 2.11-22	Proper 11, Year B	
Ephesians 3.1-12		Epiphany, ABC
Ephesians 3.14-21	Proper 12, Year B	
Ephesians 4.1-16	Proper 13, Year B	
Ephesians 4.25—5.2	Proper 14, Year B	
Ephesians 5.8-14		Lent 4, A
Ephesians 5.15-20	Proper 15, Year B	
Ephesians 6.10-20	Proper 16, Year B	

Of the 155 verses in the letter, exactly half—77 in all—are used across these seven consecutive weeks in Year B. A further quarter of the letter—38 verses—is offered for use at other seasons.

Of the remaining quarter that is not used at all, the largest portion is the so called 'Household Code' (5.21–6.9), about marriage, child-rearing and slavery. Nonetheless, this household code will be one of the issues we discuss below, because of the questions and difficulties it raises when read in our present context.

The following sections of this chapter will sketch and explore some questions that arise from particular texts in Ephesians.

Election

First, an issue that claims an early place in the text and speaks of an early moment in time. 'God chose us in Christ before the foundation of the world' (1.4). Many Christians in the past have made much of the idea of God's election, but most church people today would be more wary of the concept than these forebears were. We have learned much about the justice of God, about a God who shows no favouritism, and that seems to run counter to the idea of election (6.9).

Nonetheless, since this turn of thought is so strongly foregrounded in Ephesians, it is surely worth our pausing with the questions it raises to think what the author might have been getting at, and to ask whether there might be anything in this for us today. Here are four points to consider.

1 This first long blessing in Ephesians is a single sentence of 200 words (1.3–14). It is a grand sweep across the whole story and history of God's purposes. Its destination and climax in time is the 'summing up of all things, in heaven and on earth, within the headship of Christ' (1.10). So to speak of the beginning of God's purposes in Christ—of blessing, election, purpose, destiny, will and good pleasure—brings a symmetry, an initial bookend, to this sweep through history (1.3–5). It matters to the author that what God accomplished through the death and resurrection of Jesus and in gathering the church was not accidental but intentional, the focal point of a divine purpose that runs from beginning to end through and in Christ.

2 Thus God's electing love works 'in Christ' (1.4). The people whom the letter calls chosen are so because Christ is chosen. He is, above and in all, the elect one (John 1.34, variant text). Christians are elect 'in him' (1.4). Their chosen identity is worked out in Christ and in dependence on him. Election comes with vocation and relationship embedded in it.

3 The purpose of God's election is quite specific: 'That we might be holy and blameless before him in love' (1.4). Election is a solemn responsibility. There is no warrant for complacency—'I'm chosen, I'm all right.' Ephesians suggests that election is a challenge, a command, a calling and a commitment. 'Chosen to be holy' is no easy option. It is a representative task, embodying the presence and nature of Christ within the world.[6]

4 Election could be a dangerous doctrine for a privileged church. If one were not careful, it could function as heavenly icing on the

cake of an earthly prosperity theology, feeding complacency and even arrogance. Yet that is not the way Ephesians uses the idea. Members of the Ephesian church may well have lost position and privilege because of their faith in Jesus. They felt fragile, marginal, threatened, overshadowed. To speak, then, of God's eternal purpose sets their sacrifices and burdens in a more positive context. It strengthens resolve, and sharpens commitment, to stick with the gospel and serve the Lord.

Armed Theology

Many Christians look with a degree of ambivalence on armed conflict. Some are pacifist. A larger group would think that recourse to arms may sometimes be necessary, but it surely falls a long way short of God's ideal. Christ came to speak of peace, and we are wary about speaking for war. So how, then should Christians deal with a text about armour, sword and battle (6.10–20)? Certainly this is not the only place we meet military language in the New Testament letters. In Philippians, for example, the church is called to 'stand, strive, suffer and struggle' (Phil 1.27–30). Colossians too talks of 'good order and firm faith,' suggesting an army holding its line (Col 2.5). But this text stands out, because the metaphor is extended across so many verses.

Two insights may help. First, this is metaphor; this is not a human battle 'against flesh and blood' (6.12). Secondly, most of the armour is defensive. This church may well feel pushed about by religious and imperial powers. Here they are encouraged to 'stand.' The verb comes up in one form or another four times—'stand…stand against…stand…stand' (6.11, 13, 14). This is about holding firm, more than about fighting back.

Paul describes himself as 'chained' (6.20), yet the readers must pray for him to keep speaking with clarity and good effect; that would be an impressive kind of holding firm (6.19). Surely they too are to hold fast their Christian profession without wavering (Heb 10.23). The call in the second half of the letter for unity (4.1–16), holiness and imitation of Christ (4.17–5.20), and mutual submission requires resistance and resolve, strength of faith and character in a testing context and culture (5.21–6.9). The verbs in these chapters are plural. This task summons Christians together, to shared courage and service. That is what the language of armour is aiming to achieve.

When You Are Not at Home

Another difficult issue to address is the interpretation of the household code. One commentator says, 'I approach the following material as one might when venturing into a minefield.'[7] The code unfolds in three sections, about marriage

(5.22–33), children (6.1–4), and slaves (6.5–9). The biggest questions arise from the first and third of those sections.

On marriage, we live in a culture where equality between the sexes matters.[8] This may not be realised fully in our society, but it has gained a lot of ground in recent generations, as both a value that people embrace and a practice that is widely pursued, whereas Ephesians calls the husband 'head' of the wife and sets the wife in a role of submission (5.23f). That does not seem equal, say many; so perhaps the text is not helpful either.

Slavery was legally banned in Britain nearly two hundred ago, yet we still live with legacies of the transatlantic trade. There is a shameful and painful history to reckon with, and some of that reckoning is still incomplete. Further, we are more aware than we were a few years ago of the extent of modern slavery. I hear figures of over ten thousand modern slaves in Britain, and over forty million worldwide.[9] So what benefit can we gain from a passage that appears to accept slavery without challenge, and has indeed been used, not so very many generations ago, to support the institution of slavery and give the church's approval to a very bad practice?

For these reasons, some Christians are disinclined to invest time and thought on texts like this, particularly if these texts do not appear in their church's lectionary. Nonetheless, we ought to ask what the letter may be doing here.

This section comes directly after the call to holiness in everyday life. There is talk of honesty and goodwill in word and deed, of peacemaking and purity, of renewed character and conduct, of minds that are alert, discerning and thankful (4.17—5.20). Now, says Cohick, 'This section brought their faith down to a livable level.'[10] It takes the talk about values, and speaks of cashing these out in domestic relationships, in the household where spouses live, children grow and slaves work. This is where you are, is the implication, and this is how you can live within the situation.

The letter is dealing in realism rather than in ideals

There are expectations within the culture, and the letter does not take issue with all of these. We might wish it had. But whether that sort of advice would have had much hope of fulfilment is harder to say. Cohick talks of an honour-shame culture, where a person's respect and relationship among neighbours and in wider society came through adherence to the customs and norms of the time. In such a culture, she says, there is limited room for social manoeuvre. If we follow that train of thought, then the letter is dealing here in realism rather than in ideals, and is reckoning with patriarchy and slavery as realities that for the moment are just there.

Yet a distinctive perspective appears, in the way that each of these relationships is referred in one way or another to Christ. The whole code is prefixed with a call to mutual submission 'out of reverence for Christ' (5.21). Marital relationships are to imitate the two sides of the church's relationship with Christ (5.24f, 29). Children and parents deal with one another 'in the Lord' (6.1, 4). Slave owners answer to Christ, the same Lord to whom the Christian slave offers the work of each day (6.9, 7). In each section of the code, the party that Greco-Roman social ethics regarded as subservient is addressed first, as a responsible Christian partner. This is not symmetry, but it is more dignified, more deliberate and more mutual than was customary in the Greco-Roman world.

The Greek thinker Aristotle spoke of the husband 'ruling' the wife.[11] Ephesians does not use that verb. It talks of sacrificial love (5.25). Christian masters are to 'do the same' to their slaves, 'the same' being the respect with which those slaves are to serve the Lord (6.5–9). The call to submission at the start of the Ephesian code is comprehensive (5.21). It applies to everyone. All submit, all sacrifice, all serve.

Further, the much-discussed noun 'head' may carry a sense in Ephesians that is not narrowly hierarchical. The relationship between Christ as head and the church as body (1.22f; 4.15f) is one where life, resources and experience are generously shared, and where growth is intimate.[12] Some of that thinking is evident in 5.23 in the juxtaposition of 'head' and 'saviour.'

Gathering all of these threads of thought, there may be three lines of interpretation to consider. One is the issue of realism, of dealing with the social conventions and aspirations that we actually meet. Which might mean, for example, in a society today that tries to take seriously the equal status of women and men, that a church should work with the grain of that commitment. Some churches, including my own, seek to do so out of conviction. But perhaps, even for churches who do not share this conviction, there is an argument for doing so out of realism. There is a realistic character to the household code, as well as an orientation of that realism to Christ.

A second issue is the point about relating situations to Christ. Many people have to spend time in homes, families and workplaces that are far from ideal, in settings that embody unjust and unholy habits and expectations. I do not suggest that all of these evils are as stark and sordid as slavery. But, like ancient slavery, some of today's pressures and practices may be difficult to shift. Some situations are not going to change in a hurry. In those places phrases like 'in Christ, as to the Lord, like Christ did, for the Lord' may still be able to shape Christian living and serving, even if that life and service are in circumstances and structures that seem seriously awry.

A third line of interpretation arises from the differences noted above between conventional Greco-Roman ethics and the New Testament household codes.[13] A trajectory is coming into view, argue many readers, a direction of travel, heading towards equality. By this reading the Ephesian text points towards—even if it does not itself quite reach—a genuine and level Christian mutuality, in gender relations, in family life and in the workplace.[14]

Questions

- How, if at all, have you known the idea of election to be used in preaching and pastoral work?
- Has your understanding of your own Christian service something of election about it? Put another way, were you called to what you do? If so, how do you relate this to the experience of Christians who may not have felt that sort of calling?
- How do you relate the idea of 'the gospel of peace' to the military image of armour (6.15)?
- What benefits, if any, would you expect Christians to receive from reading and reflecting upon the Ephesian household code? Would you expect these benefits to outweigh any puzzles or problems this reading might raise for them?

Christian Experience in Ephesians 4

This third chapter aims to be more pastoral and practical in tone than those above. It seeks to draw closely on the text of Ephesians, to discover what the letter says about Christ's power and gifts, in the individual Christian and the fellowship of the church. We start by looking across the letter as a whole at the motive power for Christian living, the Holy Spirit.

The Spirit and the People of Christ[15]

The Spirit and the Christian

In the long blessing that reaches from the beginning of time to the end, the Spirit is described as 'seal' and 'pledge,' a mark of God's presence in the Christian believer, the signpost and first instalment of a closer relationship with God that will unfold in eternity (1.13–14).

The Spirit is a teacher, sharing God's wisdom with the church (1.17–19), helping Christians to understand the breadth and reach of the good news (3.5). The expression 'Spirit of wisdom' (1.17) appears in the Old Testament too, about a promised coming king (Isa 11.2). Now the one who embodies that promise, the Messiah Jesus, shares his Spirit of wisdom with the people he leads.

As well as wisdom, the Spirit is a source of strength, bringing solidity into the inner life of Christian people (3.16). The call to be strong at the end of the letter surely means drawing deep on the life of the Spirit (6.10).

The Spirit and Christian Fellowship

In Ephesians the reach of the Spirit is ecumenical and international. When Christians find rich and strong church fellowship with sisters and brothers from another tradition or nation, we echo something of the message of Ephesians. Believers in Jesus among the Jewish people and Christians from the Gentile world 'both have access in one Spirit to the Father' (2.18). The church's bond with God is inclusive. The Spirit makes it so. And the Spirit comes to live among Christ's people: the church is 'a holy temple, a dwelling place for God in the Spirit' (2.21–22).

The Spirit and Christian Behaviour

Only twice in the letter does the full name 'Holy Spirit' appear (1.13 and 4.30). In both places it is clear that Christians too are meant to be holy. Christian lives should reflect the distinct and beautiful life of God. So the words 'Holy Spirit' at 1.13 echo back to the start of the letter's long opening praise, to the thought that Christians are 'chosen to be holy, blameless and loving' (1.4). God has a purpose for the church; the Spirit comes to fulfil it.

In the same way the words 'Holy Spirit' at 4.30 challenge Christians to lead holy lives. The Spirit has feelings. God 'grieves' when Christians sin—having the Holy Spirit in us, using the name of Jesus, but living as if this were not a reality.

The Spirit and Christian Struggle

Living is a battle. We thought earlier about the armour of God; part of this armour is the word of God, that has a sharp probing edge in the hands of the Spirit (6.17). Christians talk to God, too, 'in the Spirit' (6.18). Perhaps this is shorthand for the sort of analysis we find in Romans 8: the Spirit kindles the Christian's prayer and enables this to be heard in the heart of God.

All this is the motive power that animates the church, the pattern of living into which God's Spirit constantly guides and calls us. We go on to look at the life of the church, and the life of God within it.

The Church: A Purposeful People

We spoke earlier of Artemis as the main power in Ephesus, shaping not only the religious life of the city but a great deal of its culture, its psyche, its sense of identity and community life. Against that background it would have been natural for the new church in Ephesus to feel threatened and outclassed, to be content with a small vision, a narrow personal view of the faith, and a rather privatized relationship with Jesus.

Yet Ephesians talks of the power of Christ, of the majesty and might of his resurrection and ascension, of his supremacy over every 'rule and authority and power and dominion,' and this is surely intended as a word to straighten the spine, clear the eye and lift the heart. Language of this kind offers the church a hope that its witness counts. It says to them, in effect, 'Even in a culture where you are painfully small, even in the face of arrangements and attitudes that seem to blank you out, even amid stories, superstitions, spirits and ceremonies that claim the world and leave no room for your good news—even there, your witness has power and potential.' When Christians live for Christ, follow the gospel and act as church, when the wind of the Spirit breathes through their fellowship, they are making known 'the wisdom of God' to 'the forces and authorities' that shape culture (3.10). They speak back, offer grace and wisdom, and act out an authentic pattern of living and caring.

This leads on to the affirmation at the end of chapter 3, that God, by 'the power at work within us, is able to do much, much more than all that we can ask or think' (3.20). Ephesians reckons with a God of surprises, who multiplies what believers offer; a God of alchemy, who turns the ordinary metal of Christian service into the gold of grace. That is the point to which Ephesians 3 brings us: what the church is called to do; what it is here for; what God means to do through it. Then chapter 4 speaks of how the church is called to be: what are the gifts, the hopes, the habits that will bring this about? There are three major themes: unity (4.1–6), activity (4.7–16) and holiness (4.17–5.20). The pages ahead will concentrate on the first two of these.

Unity

'I beg you to lead a life,' says Ephesians, 'worthy of the calling to which you have been called, with all humility and gentleness, with patience, bearing with one another in love, making every effort to maintain the unity of the Spirit in the bond of peace' (4.2f). The logic of this is that unity lies beneath effective witness. How Christians hold together, what they are with and for each other, shapes what they can be in the wider world and for neighbours. A church is only likely to know about care and compassion, to have skills and habits in forgiveness and peacemaking, to be attuned to the complexity and pains of neighbours' living, to want to bother, if it has learned and practised those ways of being in its own fellowship. It will not do outreach well unless its people also relate well to one another. A church that binds people together of different sorts and types, of varied backgrounds and needs, of diverse gifts and circumstances, will be a church that can look outward with hope and love, and with a sense of possibility and promise.

A further reason for treating other Christians as valuable, for shaping Christian living relationally, for reckoning the whole life of the body of Christ as greater than the sum of its parts, is that each Christian is gifted by God's Spirit. 'Each of us was given grace according to the measure of Christ's gift' (4.7). The church is a body of gifted, graced people, a fellowship where each has something precious to bring to the life and work of the whole, a family in which the presence and experience of every member is part of a broad tapestry of grace, displaying the love and reality of Jesus Christ, speaking back to everything in its ambient culture that devalues, degrades, despises or disadvantages the living of others. This leads on to the second theme of Ephesians 4.

Activity

The church is described as a people with something to offer. Christ's gifts bring momentum and direction to the life of his people. Ephesians 4 speaks about nature and nurture—what gifts are given, and how they contribute to the church's common life.

We start with nature. 'The gifts he gave were...' The different gifts, energies and patterns of service that Christ shares are gifts of the Spirit. They come from the ascension. They reflect and embody the power and spread of the love of Jesus. They echo the emphasis elsewhere in Scripture that as Jesus is ascended so the Spirit comes; as Jesus leaves his people, he does not leave them alone; as he steps aside, they discover a new energy and confidence.

'The gifts he gave were...' apostles, prophets, evangelists, pastors and teachers. 'Officials,' one writer calls them.[16] I wonder if that is quite the right word. Officials can be pretty set characters, difficult to move on, locked into formal ways of doing things. Yet this passage suggests service that might be fluid as well as formal, personal rather than narrowly procedural, concerned with the flow of the life of Christ rather than a locked-in set of habits and rules. It may involve God's surprises as much as any human systems—for God can do more than all than we ask or think.

This passage suggests service may involve God's surprises as much as any human systems

So how might the five gifts and the roles they enable contribute to the church's ongoing life? As an aside, I do think of these as enduring charisms for the church in every age. Certainly Ephesians suggests a unique historical role for the 'apostles and prophets'—even though it is difficult to define a particular group of 'prophets' in this foundational role; the 'apostles' are rather easier to identify (2.20). Yet if we ask whether it is valid to project foundational gifts forward into later generations, there is an analogy in the theme of witness to Easter. Only one group of people could do this in history, yet the church is called to do it constantly. Perhaps too an apostolic church needs to keep its apostolicity alive, by ongoing innovative and pioneering mission.

For with apostles the accent is on outreach, on noticing where God's mission might be leading, and taking the risk of following. Apostles get the gospel into new places, in word and action. They take some of the knocks that go with that outreach, and they give the rest of the church the courage and confidence to join them. There is a visionary quality to apostleship, but not an abstract vision; rather, a vision linked to action, initiative and leadership.

Prophecy, too, is a visionary gift, but it does not always carry the missionary dimension of apostleship; it is more of a church-oriented gift. If you ask what prophecy is, the New Testament gives no very simple answer. But it generally seems to mean something like this: prophets can read their times and their context; they have a sense of what is going on in the world and where God might be within it; they know how to share this insight with others; and they have some personal skills in doing so—they can speak in a way that is constructive, enabling, strengthening.

Evangelists are third in the list. They look outwards. They have the knack of commending the Christian faith to people who do not yet know Jesus as well as he knows them. They are interested in people, and can put themselves in another person's shoes and understand their concerns. They are confident enough in Jesus to want others to know him too, and can talk about their faith in ways that are inviting, accessible and attractive.

Pastors know how to support others through the thick and thin of the years. They can get alongside another person, win their confidence, and handle that confidence with integrity and respect. Pastors are used to dealing with different people in different ways; they are not fazed by awkward and wayward individuals; they are richly blessed with common sense, and they want to see the people around them living secure, wholesome and happy lives.

Finally, among the five, teachers enable others to strengthen their grip on the Christian faith. They have clear minds, honest words, the capacity to help others discover and deepen their knowledge of Christ. They listen to other people's questions. They make the faith make sense. They know how to connect Scripture and experience.

Now for three negatives, things I do not believe about those gifts.

1. They are not so narrowly concentrated that if one person is a pastor, the next person probably is not. A local church may have numerous people with pastoral gifts. No congregation need expect to find all of these gifts in its elected leaders and none of the gifts outside that group; still less are these gifts exclusive to clergy. Most clergy are good at some of these things; a few are good at several of them. But nowhere and never is that meant to set others in the shadows.
2. The churches I know best have not always been good at expressing all the gifts. We have been more comfortable with the stable than the novel, the known rather than the risky, the settled life of the church rather than the tangled life of the world. In practice our leaders have often been better as pastors and teachers than as apostles, prophets and evangelists. We might need, and perhaps some other churches might too, to review and reset that emphasis.
3. None of these gifts can be safely overlooked and bypassed. Even a local congregation needs them all. If we are not in some way apostolic, we shall never think mission: our towns will change, our times will change, and we shall not notice, because we are more interested

in the life of the church than the needs of the world. If there is no prophecy, we shall be shaped by habit rather than hope, by grooves more than grace. Without evangelists we shall have nothing to say to our neighbours; they will think us self-centred, and our faith will grow stale for lack of air. If no-one is pastoral among us, we shall ignore the needs and hurts in and around our fellowship; bruised people will fall off the edge, and those who remain will grow bitter and fractious. And without teaching we shall be all good intention without the stability of knowing why we do it.

So perhaps it would help each of us to ask if anyone in our local church is a bit of an apostle, who can spot where God's mission is leading and nudge the life of the fellowship in that direction. Who has something of the prophet about them, and helps us to believe that God is at work among and around us? Who is good at sharing the faith with outsiders, at helping neighbours to trust in our Lord? Who has the gift of caring, and communicating the compassion and companionship of Christ? And who can help us to make sense of the faith and grow in knowledge of God? We need this balance, this fivefold expression of the life of the gospel. Without it we shall not become the churches we could be, or the Christians we should be. We need to value gifts, and those through whom these gifts are given to us.

Which brings us round to the reason gifts are given: 'To equip God's holy people for the work of serving others and for building up the body of Christ' (4.12).

These three clauses are not in parallel, not on an equal footing. The short introductory words vary—'to...for...for.' So the first of the clauses—'to equip'—is the part of the verse that governs the other two. Gifts are given to equip, to repair and renew, to get in order, the life of God's holy people—in other words, to give the church energy and confidence. The energy and confidence in turn are there for two purposes—ministry and upbuilding: put another way, for service and growth. The word 'ministry' can mean humble service of other people. It calls up an image of Jesus girded with a towel, washing the disciples' feet. Christians are equipped and enabled to be generous, active, involved, busy, compassionate, committed, humble. Then the second purpose is growth—growth together as a body, as a fellowship. And we return to the theme of unity, and the witness of the church as a lively body of people, belonging together.

So the task of the church in any age is to nurture the gifts, so that the gifts may nurture us; to enable those who are gifted, so that they may enable others; to let God give to the church, that we may give to the world; to value every member of the fellowship, because they have something valuable of Christ to share; to let the gospel work among us, because God can do much more than all we can ask or think. In an era and a culture that sometimes seem to blank us out, we recognize that we have something worthy, hopeful and God-given to share, which can speak back to all that destroys and diminishes God's world.

Octopus or Bicycle?

This chapter of the booklet started, in another setting, as a talk with a question: 'The Church: Octopus or Bicycle?' Some images of the church might tend to see it as an octopus. One leg for apostleship; one for prophecy; one each for evangelism, care and teaching. And three for inertia, for wrapping around a rock, and making sure that the other five never actually accomplish anything fresh or go anywhere new. Stability, we call it; stagnation might be a better word. Maybe God is saying in our day, 'You won't go, unless you let go.'

Which brings us to the bicycle. Here, of course, you do not go unless you let go. You only get stability by moving. A stationary bike is very unstable indeed. A bike with wheels, pedals, chain, limbs, steering and even occasionally the brakes, all working together, can be stable and mobile both at the same time. It will only be one if it is the other.

The church that is octopus might get caught and conflicted between reaching out and holding on. The church that is bicycle might well find that its energy gives it stability, and stability allows it to move forward, and moving forward will in turn generate a sense of energy. All of which might reflect something of the message of Ephesians and of the life of Christ.

Questions

- Apostles, prophets, evangelists, pastors, teachers:
    - ◊ which of those gifts has been your main strength in Christian service;
    - ◊ which of those gifts is the one you personally most need to strengthen?
- As you look at your local congregation, which of those five gifts do you think is working best in the fellowship, and which is most obviously lacking? How much does that lack matter in practice?

5 Commentaries on Ephesians

As with almost every biblical book, a plethora of commentaries is available. Here are seven:

Clinton E Arnold, *Ephesians* (Zondervan Exegetical Commentary on the New Testament) (Grand Rapids, MI: Zondervan, 2010). Weighty but not inaccessible. Well researched about ancient Ephesus. Plenty of discussion of the meaning of the text and of how to apply it. Theologically the most conservative in this list.

Ernest Best, *A Critical and Exegetical Commentary on Ephesians* (International Critical Commentary) (Edinburgh: T and T Clark, 1998). Lengthy, detailed commentary by a scholar with a strong grasp of Pauline theology. Discusses the text acutely, addresses exegetical difficulties, but does not really address the preacher.

Lynn H Cohick, *Ephesians* (New Covenant Commentary) (Eugene, OR: Wipf and Stock, 2010). The slimmest commentary in this list, but written with depth and care. A rarity (for Ephesians) in having a female author. For many this would be a best buy.

Stephen E Fowl, *Ephesians: A Commentary* (New Testament Library) (Louisville, KY: WJK, 2012). This series does not allow much spreading into application. Yet the author is interested in using Scripture theologically and this responsible middle-sized commentary will be ideal for some.

Andrew T Lincoln, *Ephesians* (Word Biblical Commentary) (Dallas, TX: Word, 1990). Lots of thorough academic discussion and deep probing into a host of critical, exegetical and theological questions. But it does not really tell you how or what to preach.

Rudolf Schnackenburg, *Ephesians: A Commentary* (Edinburgh: T & T Clark, 1991). A veteran Roman Catholic scholar, who cares deeply about Christ's church and rejoices to explore theological issues. Dating a little; the German original was 1982.

Ben Witherington III, *The Letters to Philemon, the Colossians and the Ephesians: A Socio-Rhetorical Commentary on the Captivity Epistles* (Grand Rapids, MI: Eerdmans, 2007). Covers Ephesians in 150 pages. Reads it as a homily, circulated to several churches. Concerned to bridge between the realities of the ancient world and the needs of today's church.

Notes

1 N T Wright, *Paul for Everyone—The Prison Letters* (London: SPCK 2002) p 3.
2 N A Dahl, *Studies in Ephesians* (WUNT 133) (Tübingen: Mohr, 2000) p 471.
3 Paul Trebilco, *Jewish Communities in Asia Minor* (Cambridge University Press, 1991).
4 There has been much writing in recent decades about ways that the biblical authors may have reckoned with and referred to the imperial powers of their day. There is a sustained argument for the importance of this theme in Wes Howard-Brook, *'Come Out, My People.' God's Call out of Empire in the Bible and Beyond* (Maryknoll, NY: Orbis, 2010). A more cautious appraisal of the matter is offered in Scot McKnight and Joseph B Modica (eds), *Jesus is Lord. Caesar is Not: Evaluating Empire in New Testament Studies* (Downers Grove, IL: IVP, 2013).
5 In 2021, this sequence will run from 11 July to 22 August.
6 There is an extended reflection on this in Andy Johnson, *1 and 2 Thessalonians* (Two Horizons New Testament Commentary) (Grand Rapids, MI: Eerdmans, 2016) pp 316ff.
7 Lynn H Cohick, *Ephesians* (New Covenant Commentary) (Eugene, OR: Wipf and Stock, 2010) p 127.
8 I write as a British person.
9 From the websites of Anti-Slavery International and the International Justice Mission, respectively, January 2019.
10 Cohick, *op cit*, p 127.
11 Aristotle, *Politics*, 1.13
12 From Best, p 408: 'the head is regarded as the source of growth...and not as overlord or ruler'.
13 In Colossians 3.18–4.1 and 1 Peter 2.11–3.7, as well as Ephesians.
14 There is a different reading in Arnold's commentary. He argues that Paul's teaching about a husband's leadership intentionally challenges features of Ephesian culture, not least the influence there of the reverence given to Artemis (pp 372–379); also that this pattern can and should be applied to marriages today (pp 399–410). I wonder, however, if the specific link that he makes to Ephesus might undercut in some ways his call for a very wide application of the text.
15 Material in this short section is used with permission of the Group for Evangelism and Renewal in the United Reformed Church. Some of it appeared in *In GEAR*, 132 (2018).
16 This term is discussed by Best, pp 393f.